T0209742

Great Women
OF THE
Bible

DR. JOHN THOMAS WYLIE

authorHOUSE®

AuthorHouse™
1663 Liberty Drive
Bloomington, IN 47403
www.authorhouse.com
Phone: 1 (800) 839-8640

Published by AuthorHouse   09/03/2019

ISBN: 978-1-7283-2620-7 (sc)
ISBN: 978-1-7283-2619-1 (e)

Print information available on the last page.

Contents

Dedication

THIS PUBLICATION IS DEDICATED to my loving wife, Angela G. Wylie (Salem Missionary Baptist Church, Lilburn, Ga) who is my best friend and strong supporter of the ministry which God has called me. Others include: Mother Clara Penny-James Copeland (Zion Baptist Church, Nashville, Tn.) And Mother Verlene Robinson (Fourteen Avenue Missionary Baptist Church, Nashville, Tn.) two great icons in the Nashville, Tennessee community and powerful gospel singers for the Lord.

I also dedicate this publication to 1st lady Sevella Terry of Tabernacle Baptist Church, Clarksville, Tennessee who aided the prophet of the Lord in my early beginnings of ministry. To 1st Lady Wyvonne L. Hatchett (Foster Chapel Missionary Baptist Church, Nashville, Tennessee), for a kind and humble spirit-led heart.

1st Lady Tamera Gordon, of the 14th Avenue Missionary Baptist Church, Nashville, Tennessee, is an inspiration to all whom she encounters and a strong woman of God, a light shining and beacon the lost to come to Jesus. I pray that the lord holds her up for years to come.

I can not forget Mother Woods, and Mother Hussie Sykes of The First Missionary Baptist Church, Pulaski, Tennessee. (Early in my pastoral ministry). These two women are spiritual in every way and were a great help and encouragement to my early days in ministry.

I express special dedication to 1st Lady Beverly Haynes, Salem Missionary Baptist Church, Lilburn, Georgia. She is strong in the Lord, always spiritual, obedient and a shining light which inspires one God-ward.

It is my prayer that God bless and hold these women up for years and years to come as they inspire and encourage others to Jesus Christ.

Special Dedication

In Memory Of My Mother
Charlye Mae Wylie

This book is especially dedicated in the sweet momory of my living mother, The Late Charlye Mae Wylie, who was the first to plant the seeds of Christian Faith in my life. She gave so much of herself teaching me the ways of Jesus Christ early in my life. More than any other person I know, she demonstrated:

> The Fruit of Love, Joy, Peace
> Patience, Kindness, Commitment,
> Goodness, Forgiveness, Gentleness,
> Fidelity, Meekness, Humility, and
> Compassion.

I miss Mother's smile and gentle face; no one but God can fill her place. Mother, you were too sweet to be forgotten, and never will be. As long as Life and Memory last; I will always remember you.

A Poem By Charlye Mae Wylie
(A Great Mother, Missionary, Singer
and A Great Christian Woman)

"God Is With Me"

Everyday when I Rise, I say my prayers to God Who is Present and is All-Wise...
Because God is with Me, I'm Blessed... Yes! Blessed by His Presence
Because God Is With Me...

So, As I Journey through this day; at Work, School, or Play I share kind words;\
Good deeds and Smiles... Because... God Is With Me All the While.

And When my days are finally through. I say a Prayer for Me, Then I say a Prayer for You... that God Be With Us, In all we say... In all we do. God Is With You...

God Is With Me!

And when at last my life is through... God's still With Me...

As I Walk with God, Through His heavenly Pearly Gates:

Not too Soon, and not too late; Lord Be with my children: On Them I Wait.

God Is With Me!

Introduction

THE BIBLE TYPICALLY DEPICTS women as possessing a role particularly sub-par (inferior) compared to that of men. This is true for the New Testament just as the Old Testament. Yet, in Christian lands, where the gospel has been paid attention to, women have been concurred increasingly more equity with men and given a higher status in the public arena.

A large portion of us who pursue Jesus Christ never again take truly the admonitions of the Apostle Paul concerning the place of women in the home and in the church. However, we can discover in the Bible, particularly in the teachings and attitude of Jesus, implications for giving women a higher status and for as indicated by them treatment as individual persons in the sight of God.

This publication, "Great Women Of The Bible," centers around a few of the surprising women noted in the Scripture – whose battles to live with confidence and fearlessness are much the same as our own. A long way From being cardboard characters, these incredible women support us through their disappointments, failures, just as their victories. Perceive how God acted in amazing and awesome approaches to draw them- - and you- - to Himself.

Reverend Dr. John Thomas Wylie

Eve

Did Eve Ever Recover From Eden?

OR THEN AGAIN DID her visit there remain new in her brain until the day she passed on? Did the sights, sounds, and scents of heaven entice her memory decades after she encountered them? or then again did everything blur like a half-recollected dream?

Did she converse with Adam about their greenery enclosure days? Did they think back about the novelty of creation? Did they snicker, recollecting the joy and blamelessness of their bareness (nakedness)? Did they share wistfulness for their preferred places in Eden, their preferred creatures, their preferred fruits?

Or then again did Eve get peaceful when the subject of fruit came up?

Did her heart throb when she recalled what it resembled to walk around with God in the cool of the night? Did her separation from him thereafter disregard her inclination lost and - despite the fact that she was with Adam?

Did she battle with the outcomes of her choice each day of her life? Did she ever become accustomed to the troublesome, unfulfilling work that expended her waking hours? Did the torments of labor startle her and make her extremely upset in equivalent measure? Did she torment herself with steady contemplations of "If only..." and "How would I be able to have...?"

Did she reveal to her children about what she had done? Did she acknowledge duty regarding her activities? Did she perceive that the way that drove her far from God could likewise be reclaimed to him?

Did she try things out of compromise with a couple of conditional petitions? Did her heart leap when she understood that forgiveness was conceivable? Did her spirit feel lighter after she admitted what she'd done?

Did she keep on grappling with sentiments of disgrace and shamefulness in God's quality? Did her reestablished association with him feel at all like her old one? Did she turn to him for solace and quality when catastrophe struck? Did she spill out her pain to him when her child Abel was killed?

Did she request that God help her understand her sentiments toward her murderous child, Cain? Did she request assurance for her wayward child?

Did Eve die with second thoughts? Or on the other hand did she understand that God's love and forgiveness can beaten anything?

THE LESSON: God can reestablish all things.

Eve: One of a kind. As per Genesis 2:21,22. Eve is exceptional among Bible characters. Other than Adam, who was made by God each individual brought into the world after Eve was conceived of a woman. Just Eve was conceived, so to say of a man (Adam).

Deborah

A Woman Of Courage

DEBORAH'S BRAVERY, DEFINITIVENESS, AND steadfast trust in God brought about a military triumph for her people.

The cycle was as unsurprising as the dry season in a desert. Following a couple of long stretches of acquiescence, the Israelites would overlook God, disregard his laws, and fiddle with idol worship. At the point when their fiendishness achieved a basic point, God would send discipline (punishment) - as a rule as an adversary oppressor.

At the point when the adversary's standard wound up terrible, the Israelites would repent and request that God send a deliverer to lead them against their foe and out of abuse. Rebuked and humbled, the Israelites would turn back to God - for a couple of years, in any case.

The example is rehashed all through the Old Testament. Just the petitions and the seriousness of the mistreatment change starting with one story then onto the next.

Around 1200 B.C., the mistreatment became nightmarish. The Israelites wound up under the thumb of Jabin, the ruler of Canaan. Jabin's implementer (His Enforcer) was an commander named Sisera, whose powers included 900 iron chariots. Sisera and his military unleashed devastation on the Israelites for two decades.

The Israelites required a deliverer sufficiently gutsy to challenge Jabin and Sisera, and sufficiently influential to rally the Israelite powers to fight. Her name was Deborah.

Deborah was known as a prophet and a judge. Individuals looked to her to settle their debates. One day Deborah brought a man named Barak and guided him to amass a multitude of ten thousand Israelites. The Lord, she stated, would deliver the Canaanites into their hands.

The main words out of Barak's mouth uncover all that we have to think about Deborah: "I'm not going except if you go!"

Deborah's reaction is similarly telling: "OK, I'll go!" she answered. "Yet, I'm cautioning you that the LORD is going to give a woman a chance to overcome Sisera, and nobody will respect you for winning the fight" (Judges 4:9). CEV

Women Of Courage

On one dimension, it's amazing disruption of the man centric culture of the day. On another dimension, it uncovers the point of view that makes Deborah a good example to individuals all over the place. She was intensely mindful of a "woman's place" in her general public. Be that as it may, she was additionally intensely mindful of her natural endowments of initiative. She was not going to give the previous a chance to meddle with the last mentioned.

Under Deborah's initiative, Barak drove the Israelites into fight against the Canaanites. At the point when the battling was done, not one soldier in Sisera's military was left alive.

Deborah did not give the foolish reasoning of others a chance to shield her from confiding in God or utilizing her undeniable endowments. Therefore, she earned an adored spot in Israel's history.

THE LESSON: Don't give others a chance to dishearten you from utilizing you natural blessings. God can utilize those endowments to accomplish something stunning through you.

Deborah is just a solitary one of three women in the Old Testament to have a poem attributed to her (see Miriam's song in Exodus 15 and Hannah's prayer in 1 Samuel 2). Deborah's song in Judges 5 is viewed as one of the most seasoned messages in the Old Testament, perhaps going back in the twelfth century BC.

Women In The Patriarchal World

In a man centric world, women wielded colossal impact (influence) - first, in their jobs as spouses and mothers. They helped shape men who formed Israel.

Sarah prompted Abraham and influenced Isaac. Rebekah prompted Isaac and influenced Jacob. Rachel exhorted Jacob and influenced Joseph. The identities, interests, and needs of these history-molding were were woven into the DNA of Israel.

Past their spousal and maternal jobs, a portion of these women were dynamic members in God's covenant. They appreciated individual associations with God and assumed key roles in his arrangement. They were observers to his inexplicable work.

Their fingertips are everywhere throughout the early scriptural story.

Their close legendary status is amusing when you think about that their depictions in Scripture are vigorously human. These were customary, ordinary women set in exceptional conditions. Their responses to these conditions - question, dread, giggling, trust, lost hope - are painfully recognizable.

However God worked through every one of them to accomplish something wonderful and exceptional. That should give hope to all who read their accounts today.

Job's Wife

SHE MISTOOK AN INTERMISSION for an ending.

Job, afterall, is notable as the informal benefactor holy person of hopelessness, misery. Books have been expounded on the persistence of Job, the preliminaries of Job, the enduring of Job. A comparative thing can be said of Job's better half.

Job's significant other encountered a similar decimation as her better half. She excessively lost every one of the ten of her children. She also lost all of money related security. Furthermore, when agonizing boils broke out all over her significant other's body, whose activity would it say it was to solace and think about him?

No companions came to comfort Job's significant other in her wretchedness. No place in the book of Job do we discover anybody endeavoring to enable her to comprehend why a loving God would enable great individuals to suffer.

While Job and his companions examined and discussed endlessly, Job's significant other was left to grapple with her very own decisions.

Job's wife came to trust that her better half had done something to displease God-something he may not have known about - and that he was being rebuffed for it. In her very own importantly unpolished way, she encouraged her better half to put a conclusion to his anguish: "Why do you still trust in God? Why don't you curse him and die?" (Job 2:9). CEV

Those brutal words, expressed in distress, likely frequented her for an incredible remainder. Bible scholars of history through the ages have utilized them to paint her as a hardhearted wench rather than as a stinging woman whose life had been flipped around just as much as her husband's.

Maybe one might say that Job's wife had committed a miscount - a similar error a significant number of us make when we face obliteration, lose, or some different emergency's better half confused an intermission with an ending.

She presumed that her family's conditions couldn't be changed - that what was valid for her significant other amid one specific season would be valid for the remainder of their lives. She disparaged God's innovative love for his people - his capacity to bring something exceptionally, generally excellent from something, awful.

Years later, Job's wife would have the chance to think about her involvement in the solace of her home - her money related security (financial security) reestablished - encompassed by her significant other and the ten children God blessed them with after their period of suffering had passed.

Where will you be and what will you need to celebrate when your period of suffering passes? Will you endure and wait on the LORD?

LIFE LESSON: God is working out something lovely amidst your affliction.

Hagar

THE ARRANGEMENT WAS DESTINED to implode from the start.

Two women bringing up children fathered by the same man. In the same family unit.

At the point when the unavoidable pressures flared, Hagar, the hireling, ended up with couple of alternatives. She had no remaining in the family, no influence to utilize. Some time ago, she'd been the mother of Abraham's solitary beneficiary: her child Ishmael.

That changed the day Abraham's ninety-year-old spouse, Sarah, brought forth Isaac. In the blink of an eye, Hagar and Ishmael's stock fell.

As the children developed or grew older, it ended up obvious that the mixed family was anything but. At the point when Sarah discovered Ishmael playing with Isaac, she contacted her limit. She begged Abraham to send Hagar and her child away - into the unforgiving desert.

Sarah's answer more likely than not appeared to be particularly brutal in light of the conditions.

The circumstance with Hagar and Ishmael was, all things considered, one of Sarah's own creation. (It hadn't been Hagar's plan to lay down with Sarah's eighty-five-year old husband.) Yet what could Hagar do?

Abraham prayed about the issue - and afterward consented to his significant other's arrangement. He gave Hagar and Ishmael a supply of bread and water and sent them to a dubious destiny (the unforgiving desert).

After a short time, the water ran out. With no hope left either, Hagar made Ishmael as comfortable as she could in the shade of a brush and after that found a spot for herself around a hundred yards away. She couldn't stand to watch her son die.

Hagar cried. Ishmael cried. At that point a holy angel of God spoke from paradise.

Hagar, for what reason would you say you are stressed? Try not to be apprehensive. I have heard your child crying. Help him up and hold his hand, since I will make him the father of a great nation (Genesis 21:17, 18). KJV

Hagar saw an adjacent well that she hadn't seen previously. She filled her container with water and gave Ishmael a drink. God's striking arrangement proceeded for two people who had been abandoned by society.

The account postscript makes reference to that Hagar found an Egyptian woman for Ishmael to wed and that they all settled in the Paran Desert. However, that doesn't tell the entire story, nor does it completely pass on the hope that Hagar's experience offers any person who's been harmed, rejected, or deserted.

The way that God didn't protect Hagar from her first predicament didn't mean he wasn't thinking about her (see Genesis 16:1-16). Quite the opposite. He provided for Hagar in her desert experience (see Genesis 21:9-21). He gave her the solidarity to bloom in an unfriendly atmosphere. He helped her to flourish where others may have shriveled.

THE LESSON: God hears our cries. Search for proof of his provision in your life. (For additional on Hagar read Genesis Chaps. 16 and 21).

Keturah

How could any other woman hope to measure up?

To become a second wife - to supplant somebody's life partner of numerous years - is troublesome under the best of conditions. The more affectionately recollected (and beyond a reasonable doubt missed) the main wife is, the greater the test the substitution wife faces.

A touch of respect is expected for Keturah, the second spouse of Abraham.

Her forerunner was Sarah. The Sarah of Genesis popularity - the principal woman referenced in the "faith lobby of notoriety" (see Hebrews 11:11). Sarah, the incredible love of Abraham's life. Sarah, the mother of his dearest child Isaac. Sarah, whose physical excellence drew consideration of kings.

How could any other woman hope to have the right stuff (to measure up)?

In spite of the fact that the Bible is short on subtleties, proof recommends that Keturah oversaw greatly. Beginning 25:2 uncovers that Keturah bore Abraham six children. In a culture where children were for all intents and purposes money, Keturah's fruitfulness expanded Abraham's stature drastically.

God had guaranteed Abraham relatives. Keturah, as Hagar and Sarah before her, assumed a functioning role in God's covenant. What's more, she had an undeniable effect in her better half's life.

In her story, we discover trust in second life partners all over the place. Furthermore, however the Bible does not disclose to us how Keturah figured out how to locate her very own character - how she got away from Sarah's shadow - there are a couple of standards worth recalling.

1. The grieving procedure must be given its due. Regardless of whether a relationship finishes in death, separation, or changeless division, it must be lamented. The procedure will differ from person to person, yet it can't be hurried or skirted. The all the more understanding and support a second mate can appear for the

grieving process, the better shot they have of starting a relationship with a sincerely solid accomplice.

2. Keep away from direct correlation. Contending with the memory of somebody's first companion is a fool's amusement. Regardless of whether the second partner thinks about positively in specific territories, will it compensate for the zones wherein the person misses the mark? Nobody in this circumstance ought to be attracted into the snare of attempting to be "better" than the principal companion.

3. Keep up a solid feeling of self. The second life partner should never dismiss their natural gifts, qualities, and capacities. They should perceive that if anything somehow managed to transpire (or their relationship), life partner number three would have colossal shoes to fill.

LIFE'S LESSON: Though you may feel like you never entirely measure up, remember this: in God's eyes, you are his child.

Bathsheba

HER RESILIENCE AND FAITH grew in the midst of suffering and scandal.

The message from King David wasn't a welcome; it was a summons. Bathsheba had no real option except to go along (obey). With her significant other, Uriah, away on a military battle, there was nobody else to speak up for her, nobody else to put a stop to what the king had at the top of the priority list.

It likely wasn't the first run through Bathsheba's beauty had pulled in undesirable consideration. Maybe she clung to trust that King David-God's chosen pioneer of Israel - wasn't that kind of man, that he hadn't generally been keeping an eye on her while she bathed, that he had an excessive amount of uprightness to exploit the spouse of a standout amongst his most faithful officers.

How her heart more likely than not been half a month later when she needed to tell the king that she was pregnant with his child.

If God works through terrible circumstances to achieve beneficial things, he had a lot of crude material to work with in Bathsheba's life. Maybe it was this hope the conviction that God would at last improve things that spurred Bathsheba to continue.

All through Bathsheba's relationship with King David, she persevered:

a. being violated:
b. conveying the offspring of the man who violated her;
c. losing her better half who died in battle;
d. losing her infant child.

If Bathsheba's faith in God was strong to the point that she thought something great would originate from these circumstances, then she was right.

Not long after David wedded Bathsheba, God permitted their infant child, who was considered in their two-faced issue, to end up wiped out (sick) and die. Bathsheba in the long run brought forth three different children. In this manner she turned out to be a piece of the messianic line. Her name shows up in the parentage of Jesus as the mother of Solomon.

At the point when David was extremely old, Bathsheba worked with the prophet Nathan to guarantee that God's chosen successor to the royal throne, her child Solomon-acquired the crown. She defeated different groups (factions) around David's different children to verify Solomon's noteworthy reign and introduce Israel's golden age.

From defenseless violated individual to political power player, Bathsheba is a demonstration of the intensity of perseverance and faith.

LIFE'S LESSON: If you remain near God, you can bear any disaster or difficulty and develop more grounded (stronger) from its wake.

Rebekah

GOD REWARDED HER RISKS and sacrifices.

Three Generations of Infertility: A Biblical Oxymoron

Like her mother-in-law, Sarah, before her and her daughter- in-law Rachel after her, Rebekah was unable to bear youngsters for quite a while. When she at long last ended up pregnant and brought forth her twin children, Esau and Jacob, it was perceived as God's supernatural response to petition.

The pitch was audacious, to say the least.

I am Abraham's servant... I solemnly promised my master that I would do what he said. And he told me,... go back to the land where I was born and find a wife for my son from among my relatives."...

When I came to the well today, I silently prayed, "You LORD, are the God my master Abraham worships, so please lead me to a wife for his son while I am here at the well. When a young woman come out to get water, "I'll ask her to give me a drink. If she gives me a drink and offers to get some water for my camels, I'll know she is the one you have chosen."...

Now please tell me if you are willing to do the right thing for my master. Will you treat him fairly, or do I have to look for another young woman? (Genesis 24:34-49).

What woman in her right mind would say yes?

A woman who comprehended the drawback of remaining in one's customary range of familiarity, that is who.

Rebekah could have avoided any risk. Nobody would have censured her for staying with the existence she knew best. Be that as it may, taking no chances doesn't appear to have been Rebekah's style. Maybe the prospect of being stuck in one spot never realizing what she may have done or how far she may have gone-panicked her more than the obscure that accompanies saying yes when opportunity thumps. Maybe she detected that genuine satisfaction lay a long ways past her customary range of familiarity.

Rebekah was a woman whose spirit of adventure couldn't be dulled by "what uncertainties (what ifs)."

Imagine a scenario where her future husband ended up being troll-like in appearance. Consider the possibility that he didn't locate her appealing. Consider the possibility that she experienced difficulty coexisting with his family or fitting in with his people. Given time and a second-speculating nature, Rebekah may have worked herself out of her descision. Rather, she heeded her gut feelings and go out on a limb a mammoth (she took a giant leap of faith).

At long last, Rebekah was a woman who comprehended that God has delights and rewards-our dangers and sacrifices.

Where God's arrangement (plan) is concerned, God's Spirit is grinding away. It's no stretch to trust that Rebekah heard God's voice-or if nothing else felt a feeling of peace from him about her decision. The inquiry was, would she tune in to God's inciting or enable common sense and circumspection to direct her?

Consistently, every day with the Lord is an adventure. The individuals who appreciate it to the fullest are:

* dependably up for a test; (always up for a challenge)

* unafraid of a little hazard (risk);
* unattached to their customary ranges of familiarity (comfort zones).

Rebekah was compensated with an adoring family, an actual existence of adventure, a role in God's covenant, and a revered place in Jewish history.

What does God have coming up for you?

LIFE LESSON: Step out of your usual range of familiarity (comfort zone) and go for a few risks with God. His ways are not our ways, however they are in every case good. (For additional on Rebekah read Genesis 24).

Leah

THE LOOK OF DISAPPOINTMENT on Jacob's face must have stayed with Leah for the rest of her life.

He had expected to discover Rachel in his wedding bed, l not her most seasoned sister. Jacob had consented to labor for a long time for Laban as an end-result of the respect of wedding his daughter Rachel.

Laban's choice to switch girls ultimately falls somewhere close to a down to earth joke and out and out extortion. Gotten amidst Laban's misdirection was Leah.

Jacob's passion for Rachel was great to the point that he consented to work an additional seven years for Laban so as to wed her. As indicated by Genesis 29:31, "Jacob loved Rachel more than he did Leah." Are there progressively more brutal or severe words in all Scripture?

However Leah the Unloved continued on. She would not acknowledge her additionally ran status. She declared her rights and benefits as a spouse. She couldn't make Jacob love her, yet she could - and made herself a fundamental piece of his life.

She reinforced her situation as Jacob's significant other by bearing and bringing up children. Delivering beneficiaries was indispensable to a man's remaining in the ancient world. Sadly, Leah's sister Rachel was desolate, barren (or so it appeared).

Leah, the notorious unnecessary extra person wheel, abruptly had footing. Truth be told, she on the grounds that imperative to Jacob. She brought forth six children speaking to a large portion of the twelve clans of Israel-and one little daughter. From Leah's third son, Levi, came Israel's line of priests. From her fourth son, Judah, came Jesus, the Messiah. Plainly, Leah was no also-ran in God's eyes.

Have you at any point been chosen last for a group or a team, disregarded for an advancement, dominated by an opponent, made to feel like a second decision, or tormented by poor self-esteem? Anybody can take support from Leah's story.

By finding for some hidden meaning in Genesis, we may much suspect that Leah would not be pummeled by the limitation and lack of interest of others. She perceived her incentive in

God's eyes and utilized that as the foundation for her mental self-image.

Honored In Death

Before his death, Jacob instructed his sons to bury his body in Machpelah Cave. This is where Abraham, Sarah, Isaac, and Rebekah had been buried (Genesis 49:29-31). NIV This was also where Jacob chose to bury Leah. Rachel, however, had died in childbirth in Canaan and had to be buried during the course of the journey (35:19; 48:7).

LIFE LESSON: Your status isn't what characterizes you. As God's child you are of great worth.

Genesis 29:21-25 – Jacob said to Leban, "The time is up, and I want to marry Rachel now!" NIV So Laban gave a big feast and invited all their neighbors. But that evening he brought Leah to Jacob, who married her and spent the night with her. Laban also gave Zilpah to Leah as her servant woman.

The next morning Jacob found out that he had married Leah, and he asked Laban, "Why did you do this to me? Didn't I work to get Rachel? Why did you trick me?"

(Want more information on Leah, read Genesis 29).

Jochebed

SHE BOLDLY TRUSTED GOD to work out the details in her life.

Nothing about Jochebed's unassuming beginnings indicated the enormity that would originate from her. She was conceived in captivity in Egypt. Her people were slave workers. To monitor the quickly developing slave populace, Pharaoh requested that all Hebrew young men be killed when they were conceived.

Presently, Jochebed brought forth an infant child.

Her much older son, Aaron, had been conceived before Pharaoh's pronouncement. Her daughter, Miriam, was unaffected, as the declaration focused on young men. Jochebed's more youthful child, be that as it may, was gotten in the focus (crosshairs).

When all else fails, compromise is unavoidable. So Jochebed made a waterproof crate (basket) for her infant and set him in the Nile River, close where Pharaoh's daughter normally washed. It was a daring arrangement, however one that attempted to flawlessness.

Pharaoh's daughter found the child and chose to keep him as her own. A deliberately situated Miriam offered to locate a Hebrew woman to provide medical attendant and care for the child, whom Pharaoh's daughter later named Moses.

Pharaoh's little daughter, meet Jochebed.

Moses' brisk reasoning (quick-thinking) mother had the option to keep up a nearness and influence in her child's life, even as he was raised by the Egyptian royal family. In the end, that influence would shake Egypt to its center and help move the level of influence in the ancient world.

Intensity and hazard were signs of Jochebed's life. Regardless of whether these qualities were because of conditions or identity involves theory. The Bible uncovers minimal about Moses' mother.

What is important is that when her children, Moses and Aaron, stood before Pharaoh to demand the release of the Hebrew people, they had Jochebed's case of intensity and boldness to draw on.

What's more, when Moses and Aaron's sister, Miriam, joined her siblings in driving the whole

Hebrew country out of Egypt-far from Pharaoh's seeking after armed force, through a separated sea, over an immense wild, and toward an obscure goal despite steady restriction she was at that point acquainted with hazard, on account of her mother.

Moses, Aaron, and Miriam were exceptionally able to lead the Exodus from Egypt to some degree, since they had a mother who was not substance to take no chances.

LIFE LESSON: We have no clue what God will do through our basic lives. Be happy to be striking and go out on a limb, and trust God to work out the subtleties.
(SEE EXODUS 2).

Rachel

THE CHOICES RACHEL MADE changed History.

Rachel had a lot of motivations to like herself. She was intelligent (see the "Like Father, Like Daughter" beneath). She was appealing. (Her looks positively turned Jacob's head). She was loved. (Jacob worked seven years for her father only for the benefit of wedding her. At the point when Rachel's father, Laban, bamboozled Jacob at last, Jacob needed to work seven additional years for Rachel's hand).

Like Father, Like Daughter

Rachel appears to have acquired a theft quality from her father. As Jacob and his family were moving out of Laban's family, Rachel stole a portion of her father's idols and shrouded them in her camel's seat pad.

Laban pursued down Jacob's parade and looked everybody and wherever for his objects of worship. Jacob unconscious of what Rachel had done, called down a scourge of death on any individual who had the idols. At the point when the opportunity arrived to look through Rachael's camel, she would not descend. She guaranteed she was having her period (Genesis 31:33-35). NIV

However Rachel couldn't discover satisfaction. Her focused soul wouldn't permit it. The issue was her sister Leah, also called the wrench in progress.

On the night Rachel was to wed Jacob, Laban substituted her more seasoned sister, Leah. Jacob didn't understand he'd been deceived until after the wedding night.

So Leah wedded Rachel's genuine love before Rachel did. Bit of leeway: Leah.

After Jacob wedded Rachel as well, he clarified that he loved her, not Leah. Preferred position: Rachel.

All things considered, Jacob split his husbandly obligations between his two spouses. Over the span of those obligations, Rachel found that she was desolate (barren). Leah, then again, found that she was very ripe (fertile). She brought forth Reuben, Jacob's firstborn child; and Simeon, his second child; and Levi, his third child; and Judah, his fourth child. Favorable position: Leah.

Rachel's focused drive kicked into overdrive. Seriously envious of her sister, she requested that her significant other give her children. Jacob countered that God was the One who was shielding her from having children.

So Rachel exchanged methodologies. She trained Jacob to lay down with her hireling Bilhah. Bilhah got pregant-twice-and Rachel guaranteed every child as a triumph for herself. She named Bilhah's first child Dan and the second child Naphtali.

In case you're looking for understanding into the character and inspiration of Rachel, look no more distant than the importance of the name Naphtali-"my struggle." Rachel said to herself, "I've struggled hard with my sister, and I've won!" (Genesis 30:8). CEV

The preferred position didn't keep going long. Leah demanded that Jacob lay down with her worker Zilpah a relationship that created two additional children.

Leah herself gave Jacob three additional children two sons and a daughter, for an aggregate of seven.

Rachel at long last countered with two offspring of her own: Joseph and Benjamin.

Such a great amount for her determination of fruitlessness.

That is the place the challenge finished. Rachel left behind a husband and two children. Her turbulent life and apparently unexpected passing may make us pose a few unanswerable inquiries:

* How a lot more joyful would her life have been on the off chance that she'd had the option to accommodate her focused impulses with her better nature?
* What on the off chance that she'd treated her sister like a colleague rather than as a rival?
* What if every one of the thirteen births in Jacob's family had been cause for festivity and not envy?
* What if Rachel had comprehended that challenge and competition ought to draw out the best-not the most exceedingly terrible in individuals?

LIFE LESSON: God can utilize standard, defective individuals to change the course of history. (For additional on Rachel see Genesis 29).

Jael

Of all the tents in all the plains in the entire ancient world, Sisera walked into hers.

Jael remembered him right away. A heartless Canaanite leader (a military commander) who had threatened Israel for a long time with a multitude of iron chariots will undoubtedly establish a connection. Gone, be that as it may, were his war machines and troops.

Sisera remained in Jael's tent, alone and powerless, yet still sufficiently pompous to request her neighborliness. Jael was very much anxious to oblige. She tended to the Canaanite's needs until he at long last let down his guard. That is the point at which she made her turn. Utilizing a mallet (hammer) and a tent peg, Jael put Sisera out of Israel's hopelessness.

Hardly any will ever be called to accomplish something as extraordinary as what Jael did. Yet any individual who tries to be utilized by God can gain from her precedent.

Jael perceived a paradise sent open door when she saw it.

God prepares and gets ready people to serve him. Jael might not have known precisely what he had available for her, however she was prepared when it came. The vast majority would have been alarmed or shaken by Sisera's interruption. Jael appears to have perceived that God placed her in the opportune spot at the ideal time.

Jael drew from a well of fearlessness she might not have realized she had.

Sisera was an edgy, perilous man. he was likewise a prepared military officer. Murdering individuals was an aspect of his responsibilities portrayal. However no place in the scriptural story does it recommend that Jael feared him. Such boldness originates from God alone. Jael was savvy enough to take advantage of it.

Jael acted definitively.

She didn't send for assistance. She didn't leave the activity to somebody increasingly experienced or more qualified for the job. She made a move herself. As David - another great warrior-would do years after the fact, Jael got the main weapons she could find and brought down a hugely scary adversary.

Deborah, the Israelite prophet and judge who knew some things about acting conclusively while being utilized by God, observed Jael in melody. In her words, we locate the ideal inscription for the woman who put a conclusion to one of Israel's main oppressors: "Yet respect Jael... give more respect to her than to some other woman" (Judges 5:24). KJV

LIFE LESSON: God has prepared and set you up for an incredible reason. Attract on his solidarity to achieve the assignments he gives you, anyway extraordinary they may appear.

- A Moral Dilemma -

Jael's lethal activity - however for a respectable reason-disregarded antiquated neighborliness rules, particularly given the peace arrangement between her family and the Canaanites.

This story isn't just about being prepared for an outrageous assignment; it is undeniably more truly about extraordinary moral and good issues; legitimate manslaughter, vow and guideline breaking, the rule of twofold impact (accomplishing something characteristically wrong for a bigger decent), and the job of individual inner voice in good judgment, and Jael could have basically handed him over.

(See More on Jael, read Judges 4).

Judges 4:16b-22 (Paraphrased).

Sisera's whole armed force was cleared out. Just Sisera got away. He hurried to Heber's camp, on the grounds that Heber and his family had peace treaty bargain with the ruler of Hazor. Sisera went to the tent that had a place with Jael, Heber's significant other. She turned out to welcome him and stated, "Come in, sir! If it's not too much trouble entered. Try not to be apprehensive."

After they had headed inside, Sisera set down, and Jael secured him with a cover. "Would I be able to have a little water?" he inquired. "I'm parched."

Jael opened a calfskin bottle and poured him some milk, at that point she concealed him back. "Remain at the passage to the tent, Sisera advised her. "On the off chance that somebody stops by and inquires as to whether anybody is inside, let them know "No."

Sisera was depleted and before long fell sleeping soundly. Jael took a mallet (hammer) and drove a tent-peg through his head into the ground, and he died.

In the interim, Barak had been following Sisera, and Jael went out to meet him. "The man you're searching for is inside," she said. "Come in and I'll show him to you."

They headed inside, and there was Sisera - dead and extended (stretched-out) with a tent - peg through his skull.

Ruth

SHE CHOSE SELF-SACRIFICE OVER self-preservation.

The circumstance was desperate. Naomi had lost her significant other and her only two children. Her daughters- in-law, Orpah and Ruth, had lost their husbands. The three women were genuinely crushed as well as physically powerless.

Gone was any suspicion that all is well and good or prosperity they have had. In a patriarchal culture and without any husbands or children to accommodate them, they were helpless before others.

Naomi, an Israelite living in Moab, chose to return to her country (her homeland) to live out her last years. Orpah and Ruth, both Moabites, offered to go with her; however Naomi realized she had no future to offer them, so she encouraged them to stay in Moab with their very own people.

Orpah and Ruth gauged their alternatives cautiously. Their very prospects were in question. Orpah chose her best game-plan was to remain in Moab. Maybe she wanted to locate another husband there.

Ruth chose to go with Naomi to Judah.

At the point when self-preservation was simply the sheltered play, Ruth picked self-sacrifice. Her inspiration was to make the best choice, regardless of whether it profited her or not. Maybe Ruth could detect that Naomi was wavering on the precarious edge of extreme wretchedness.

Maybe Ruth was worried that Naomi wouldn't most likely deal with herself. Whatever the reason, Ruth put aside her own inclinations, her own solace, and her very own desires for the future so as to make life increasingly endurable for Naomi.

In Judah, the two women attempted to endure - that is, until they met Boaz, a well off (wealthy) relative of Naomi's late husband. With regards to antiquated convention, Boaz consented to purchase land that had belonged to Naomi. As a component of the exchange, he additionally consented to wed Ruth and proceed with Naomi's family line. Among the relatives of Ruth and Boaz was the Messiah.

Back in Moab, Ruth remained to pick up nothing from her conciliatory choice. Ruth ensured that Naomi was taken care of, and thus God ensured that Ruth was taken care of.

LIFE LESSON: God takes care of the individuals who take care of others.

Ruth 1:14-18 (Paraphrased). Orpah kissed her relative farewell however Ruth clutched her. Naomi at that point said to Ruth, "Look your sister-in-law is returning to her people and to her divine beings! For what reason don't you go with her?"

Ruth replied, "Kindly don't guide me to abandon you and return home! I will go where you go, I will live where you live; your people will be my people, your God will be my God. I will die where you die and be buried beside you. May the LORD punish me in the event that we are ever separated, even by death!"

At the point when Naomi saw that Ruth had decided to go with her, she quit encouraging her to return.

(For additional on Ruth see Ruth 1 – 4).

Miriam

MIRIAM LEARNED A TOUGH lesson about jealousy and sibling rivalry.

Miriam filled in as a representative (a spokesman) for God. She was acclaimed as a prophet and perceived as a pioneer of the Israelites. Miriam is even credited with approving the absolute soonest messages in the Bible.

All things considered, the principal line of bio definitely peruses, "Miriam, the sister of Moses..."

Miriam's destiny was to serve nearby (and in the shadow of) a standout amongst Israel's most dearest prophets. That she was additionally Moses' more seasoned sister entangled the circumstance significantly further.

Miriam led the Israelites in love and worship.

Moses led them through a parted Red Sea.

Miriam composed a melody to recognize (commemorate) Israel's departure from Egypt.

Moses spoke up close and personal with God.

Miriam was respected.

Moses was revered.

Moses, Moses, Moses!

Miriam's long-stewing disappointment and jealousy reached a crucial stage when Moses wedded a Cushite woman. Detecting (mistakenly, as it turned out) that the marriage was hostile to God, Miriam tested her sibling's initiative. She requested equivalent charging for herself and their brother Aaron.

Moses didn't respond to his sister's test. He didn't have to. God's reaction was quick and definitive. He clarified that while Miriam and Aaron had the endowment of prophecy, Moses was his chosen one.

For testing Moses' authority, God hit Miriam with a malady (leprosy) that turned her skin white with disease. Moses mediated for her benefit, and in the long run God recuperated her. In any case, the point had been made.

Jealously harms everybody it contacts. Much more dreadful, it harms an individual's ministry. Miriam couldn't turn on an envious eye toward Moses' prominent service (high profile) without dismissing her own.

Likewise, Miriam overlooked the main issue that Moses had been uncommonly skilled to manage the weight and obligation, and responsibility that accompanied his position of authority similarly as she had been extraordinarily talented to satisfy her own ministry calling.

Regardless of whether Miriam could have swapped jobs with Moses, she wouldn't have discovered joy in it. That wasn't the undertaking to which she was called. Miriam took in this lesson the most difficult way possible. Wise individuals will learn from her example.

LIFE LESSON: God designed you to find satisfaction and fulfillment in his one-of-a-kind plan for your life. Envy only interferes with this experience.

Departure 15:19-21. The LORD covered the royal Egyptian rangers and chariots with the sea, after the Israelites had walked securely through on dry ground. Miriam the sister of Aaron was a prophet. So the took her tambourine and led different women out to play their tambourines and to dance. At that point she sang to them: "Sing praises to the LORD for his incredible triumph (His Great Victory)! He has thrown the horses and their riders into the sea."

(For additional on Miriam, read Exodus 15, Numbers 12).

Huldah

SHE SPOKE GOD'S TRUTH with boldness.

To state that Israel had floated (drifted) from God's plans in the prior years King Josiah would be a titanic modest representation of the truth. The country had drifted up until now, truth be told, that a great many people were ignorant or unconcerned-that God even had an plan for them.

At the point when the scrolls that contained God's laws were found in the sanctuary (temple) in Jerusalem, they more likely than not appeared unusual, old antiques.

To everybody except King Josiah and the prophet Huldah, that is.

Josiah had inherited the royal throne as an eight-year-old from his shrewd father. He was resolved to part from family tradition and lead the country back to its God-respecting ways.

In the wake of ruling for a long time (eighteen years), Josiah requested that "The Book of God's law," which was new found, be read out loud to him. What he heard staggered him. The sheer greatness of Israel's traitorousness to God wound up evident. The king tore his imperial robes in anguish and disgrace. He understood that Israel was sitting unequivocally in the focus of God's judgment.

Edgy, the ruler sent a designation to Huldah, God's prophet in Jerusalem, to discover exactly how grim the circumstance was.

Huldah's reaction uncovered three significant parts of her character-and it fills in as a model to everybody who might speak the Lord's truth.

Huldah was strong, verging on valiant.

Huldah was unfraid to talk straightforwardly to the country's above all else. To see how the prophet could have been so intense, we need just see her words to the assignment: "You were sent here by King Josiah, and this is the thing that the LORD God of Israel says to him: "Josiah, I am the LORD!" (II Kings 22:15).

Huldah was doing God's will and speaking his truth, which implied she was upheld by his power. Whom did she need to fear?

She didn't sugarcoat God's Word.

God had been resisted, disregarded, and ignored for ages. There was a cost to be paid-a horrible cost. Huldah's message would not be prominent with the general public. However she conveyed each word. She thought profoundly about her country, yet her first obligation was to enable them to comprehend God's Word, not to make them feel warm and fluffy inside.

She offered hope and a sign of renewal.

Where there is authentic contrition, there is kindness and absolution. This message of expectation is implanted all through the Bible. Huldah disclosed to Josiah that his endeavors to make compensation had won Israel a respite. For whatever length of time that he was above all else, the country would appreciate peace.

LIFE LESSON: Christians who grasp the test of offering God's message to others would be wise to pursue Huldah's example.
(For more on Huldah, read II Kings 22).

The Queen Of Sheba

THE QUEEN OF SHEBA was drawn to Solomon's renowned wisdom.

Word achieved the kingdom of Sheba (current Yemen) about a ruler in the north whose wisdom outperformed that of any who had preceded him. Voyaging traders talked in wonder of Solomon, the youthful ruler of Israel who had a practically powerful capacity to reveal reality and settle on astute choices in even the most mind boggling circumstances.

In the royal residence of Sheba, a woman of obviously glorious bearing took an exceptional enthusiasm for these records. Updates on Solomon aroused her advantage. Where different rulers may have seen a danger, the ruler of Sheba saw opportunity.

As a ruler responsible for settling on troublesome choices consistently, she valued the estimation of knowledge and comprehended its shortage. on the off chance that the reports were valid, the youthful ruler and his kingdom would make perfect partners for Sheba.

The ruler was not going to acknowledge the accounts she heard without needing any proof. It was one thing to inspire ordinary people; it was very another to awe sovereignty. The ruler of Sheba had likely gotten specific preparing since youth and was very acclimated with the organization of scholarly consultants.

The ruler chose the most ideal approach to decide if the accounts were genuine was to lead a royal convoy to Israel and test the king's amazing wisdom herself. She arranged a rundown of inquiries that would have puzzled Mensa individuals and Jeopardy! challengers alike.

At the point when the ruler of Sheba touched base in Israel, she found that Solomon more than satisfied his advance billing. The youthful ruler aced the tests without contemplating. The ruler of Sheba was overpowered by his insight and by his whole kingdom. She raved about his initiative.

Critically, the ruler was savvy enough herself to perceive God's hand in Solomon's life, and she offered praise to the Lord. To Solomon she gave uncommon flavors, valuable gems, and 9,000 pounds of gold.

More than that, however, the ruler of Sheba gave Solomon believability (credibility). Her visit and her resulting underwriting helped polish Solomon's notoriety all through the ancient world.

LIFE LESSON: You might be ruler of your world and at the highest point of your game, however, you can in any case learn from others.

I Kings 10. The Queen of Sheba heard how well known Solomon was, so she went to Jerusalem to test him with troublesome inquiries. She brought a few of her authorities and she stacked her camels with blessings of flavors, gems, and gold.

When she arrived, she and Solomon discussed all that she could consider. He addressed each inquiry, regardless of how troublesome it was. The Queen was astounded at Solomon's knowledge.

She was short of breath when she saw his castle, the sustenance on his table, his authorities, his workers in their regalia, the general population who served his nourishment, and the sacrifices he offered at the LORD'S sanctuary.

She stated: "Solomon, in my own nation I had found out about your wisdom and everything you've done. In any case, I didn't trust it until I saw it with my own eyes!

Furthermore, there's so much I didn't find out about. You are more wise and more extravagant than I was told. Your spouses and authorities are fortunate to be here where they can tune in to the savvy things you state.

I praise the LORD your God. He is satisfied with you and has made you ruler of Israel. The LORD has constantly loved Israel, so he has given them a king who will govern reasonably and sincerely."

Mary

SHE RESPONDED TO AN unbelievably heavy responsibility with humility, willingness, and joy.

To be chosen as mother of the Messiah - to bring forth the deliverer of God's people - would have been the most astounding calling comprehensible to the women of first century Israel.

Why, at that point, did that respect tumble to a poor, socially insignificant, unmarried youthful virgin named Mary?

Telling intimations can be found in her experience with the heavenly angel Gabriel. Heavenly angel appearances were uncommon occasions, even in scriptural occasions. A heavenly angel appearance to enlist the mother of the Savior was totally extraordinary. There's no standard convention for reacting appropriately to such a visit.

However Mary's response satisfied the Lord incredibly.

First, she was disrupted by Gabriel's greeting of "You are truly blessed! The Lord is with you" (Luke 1:28) CEV. Her quietude evidently did not enable her to consider herself in such shining terms.

Second, when she was determined what the Lord wanted to do, her reaction was, "I am the Lord's servant" (Luke 1:38). She was prepared to do whatever God asked of her, regardless of how it influenced her personally.

Third, Mary couldn't contain her joy. She offered a melody of commendation (praise) to pass on her fervor, her excitement and appreciation (Luke 1:46-55). This was no triumph serenade, however. Mary appears to have comprehended that her calling brought substantial duty just great responsibility) as honor.

In the months and years that pursued, Mary would need to:

* persevere through malignant tattle of rumormongers twisted on pulverizing her reputation.
* witness her child being rejected by the people who knew him best;

* listen in to derisive allegations hurled at Jesus by religious pioneers she once respected;
* stand by defenselessly as her son was strutted through the boulevards of Jerusalem with an overwhelming cross on his back.
* watch as Jesus' hands and feet were nailed to the cross, as he was spit on and taunted, as he battled for his last breath, and as a soldier push a lance (spear) into his side to ensure he was dead.

Mary had no clue why God would choose her for such significant work, yet she was resolved to see it through-praising him at the same time.

Indeed, even after her son died, rose again, and, ascended into heaven. Mary chose to praise him and follow him (See Acts 1:14).

LIFE LESSON: If you maintain a humble spirit, a servant's heart, and an attitude of joy, you will have limitless potential in God's eyes.

A Risk Worth Taking

In her pregnancy, Mary gambled significantly more than a harmed or damaged reputation. She took a chance with her very life. As per the law, a Jewish woman who neglected to remain a virgin before marriage could be stoned to death (see Deuteronomy 22:20, 21).

Bibliography

The Holy Bible (1964) Authorized King James Version. Chicago, Ill.: J. G. Ferguson

The Holy Bible (1953) The Revised Standard Version. Nashville, TN.: Thomas Nelson & Sons (Used By Permission)

The Holy Bible (1982) New International Version. Grand Rapids, MI.: Thomas Nelson, Inc. (Used By Permission)

The Holy Bible (1901) The American Standard Version. Nashville, TN.: Thomas Nelson (Used By Permission)

The Holy Bible (1959) The Berkeley Version. Grand Rapids, MI.: Zonderevan (Used By Permission)

The New Testament In The Language Of The People (1937, 1949) Chicago, Ill.: Charles B. Williams, Bruce Humphries, Inc, Moody Bible Institute (Used By Permission)

The Wycliff Bible Commentary (1962) Nashville, TN.: The Southwestern Company, The Moody Bible Institute of Chicago

About The Author

THE REVEREND DR. JOHN Thomas Wylie is one who has dedicated his life to the work of God's Service, the service of others; and being a powerful witness for the Gospel of Our Lord and Savior Jesus Christ. Dr. Wylie was called into the Gospel Ministry June 1979, whereby in that same year he entered The American Baptist College of the American Baptist Theological Seminary, Nashville, Tennessee.

As a young Seminarian, he read every book available to him that would help him better his understanding of God as well as God's plan of Salvation and the Christian Faith. He made a commitment as a promising student that he would inspire others as God inspires him. He understood early in his ministry that we live in times where people question not only who God is; but whether miracles are real, whether or not man can make a change, and who the enemy is or if the enemy truly exists.

Dr. Wylie carried out his commitment to God, which has been one of excellence which led to his earning his Bachelors of Arts in Bible/Theology/Pastoral Studies. Faithful and obedient to the call of God, he continued to matriculate in his studies earning his Masters of Ministry from Emmanuel Bible College, Nashville, Tennessee & Emmanuel Bible College, Rossville, Georgia. Still, inspired to please the Lord and do that which is well – pleasing in the Lord's sight, Dr. Wylie recently on March 2006, completed his Masters of Education degree with a concentration in Instructional Technology earned at The American Intercontinental University, Holloman Estates, Illinois. Dr. Wylie also previous to this, earned his Education Specialist Degree from Jones International University, Centennial, Colorado and his Doctorate of Theology from The Holy Trinity College and Seminary, St. Petersburg, Florida.

Dr. Wylie has served in the capacity of pastor at two congregations in Middle Tennessee and Southern Tennessee, as well as served as an Evangelistic Preacher, Teacher, Chaplain, Christian Educator, and finally a published author, writer of many great inspirational Christian Publications such as his first publication:

"Only One God: Who Is He?" – published August 2002 via formally 1st books library (which is now AuthorHouse Book Publishers located in Bloomington, Indiana & Milton Keynes, United Kingdom) which caught the attention of **The Atlanta Journal Constitution Newspaper.**

Dr. Wylie is happily married to Angel G. Wylie, a retired Dekalb Elementary School teacher who loves to work with the very young children and who always encourages her husband to move forward in the Name of Jesus Christ. They have Four children, 11 grandchildren and one great-grandson all of whom they are very proud. Both Dr. Wylie and Angela Wylie serve as members of the Salem Baptist Church, located in

Lilburn, Georgia, where the Reverend Dr. Richard B. Haynes is Senior pastor.

Dr. Wylie has stated of his wife: "she knows the charm and beauty of sincerity, goodness, and purity through Jesus Christ. Yes, she is a Christian and realizes the true meaning of loveliness as the reflection as her life of holy living gives new meaning, hope, and purpose to that of her husband, her children, others may say of her, "Behold the handmaiden of the Lord." A Servant of Jesus Christ!

About The Book

THIS PUBLICATION, "GREAT WOMEN Of The Bible," clarifies seventeen rousing and surprising women noted in the Scripture - whose battles to live with "Faith" and "Valor" are much the same as our own.

A long way from being cardboard characters, these extraordinary women support us through their disappointments just as their triumphs. Perceive how God acted in astounding and great approaches to draw them-- and you-- to "Himself."

Slow your reading and appreciate the story of God's love for his people, offering a crisp point of view that will nourish and fortify your own fellowship with him.

This publication does not address all the women of the Bible only a chosen few of courage and valor. Nevertheless, I'm sure you will appreciate its spiritual encouragement.

Reverend Dr. Wylie is devoted to publishing books that spread the good news of Jesus Christ, helping Christians to live as per that gospel, advance restoration, revival in the congregation, and give testimony regarding Jesus Christ, Christian Unity, and Fellowship in Love.

Reverend Dr. John Thomas Wylie

Printed in the United States
By Bookmasters